Unlocking The Book of REVELATION

By

Patti Hanni

Pearson Jagoe Publishing
Denison, Texas
2020

Copyright © 2020 by Patti Hanni, Denison, Texas.

All rights reserved. No part of this book may be reproduced in any form or by any means without permission from Patti Hanni.

ISBN-13 978-1-7327206-0-2

Library of Congress Control Number: 2020921041

Credits:

Unless otherwise noted, all scripture references and quotations are from the New King James Study Version of the Bible. Copyright 1997, 2007 by Thomas Nelson, Inc.

Background information was obtained from Spiritual Warfare Bible. Copyright 2014 by Passio Charisma Media/Charisma House Book Group, and based on The Holy Bible, Modern English Version, copyright 2014 by Military Bible Association.

Front cover photograph by Patti Hanni

Cover production and technology support: Robert Wayne Massey

Published by:

Pearson Jagoe Publishing
600 Ambassador Street
Denison, Texas. 75020
www.PearsonPub.US
info@pearsonpub.us

2020

Table of Contents

Preface v

Author's Note vii

Map: The Seven Churches of Revelation ix

Chart: The Seven Seals of Revelation xi

Revelation: Introduction 1

Chapter 1 3
    John's Greeting to the Seven Churches 3

Chapter 2 7
    The Message to the Church of Ephesus 7
    The Message to the Church in Smyrna 10
    The Message to the Church in Thyatira 13

Chapter 3 17
    The Message to the Church in Sardis 17
    The Message to the Church in Philadelphia 18
    The Message to the Church in Laodicea 19

Chapter 4 23
    Message for the Church 23
    Worshipping God in Heaven 23

Chapter 5 27
    The Lamb Opens the Scroll 27

Chapter 6 31
    Opening the Seven Seals 31
    The Lamb Breaks the First Six Seals 31

Chapter 7 35
    God's People Will Be Preserved 35
    Praise From the Great Multitude 36

Chapter 8 39
    The Lamb Breaks the Seventh Seal 39

Chapter 9 43
    The Fifth Trumpet Brings the First Terror 43
    The Sixth Trumpet Brings the Second Terror 44

Chapter 10 47
    The Angel and the Small Scroll 47

Chapter 11... 51
    The Two Witnesses..51

Chapter 12... 55
    Observing the Great Conflict..55
    The Woman and the Dragon..55

Chapter 13... 61
    The Beast Out of the Sea...61

Chapter 14... 67
    The Lamb and the 144,000..67

Chapter 15... 71
    Pouring Out the Seven Plagues...71
        The Song of Moses and of the Lamb..71

Chapter 16... 73
    The Seven Bowls of the Seven Plagues..73

Chapter 17... 77
    Seizing the Final Victory...77
    The Great Prostitute...77

Chapter 18... 81
    The Fall of Babylon..81

Chapter 19... 85
    Songs of Victory in Heaven..85
    The Rider on the White Horse...86

Chapter 20... 89
    The Thousand Years..89
    The Defeat of Satan...90
    The Final Judgement...91

Chapter 21... 95
    Making All Things New..95
    The New Jerusalem...95

Chapter 22... 101
    Jesus Is Coming..102

Conclusion... 105

Final Blessing... 107

PREFACE

A few years ago, a friend asked me to explain what the seven lampstands represent in Revelation. As I researched and explained to the best of my ability, my friend said, 'you should write a study on Revelation.' Well, that went in one ear and out the other although it has come to my mind many times since then.

A week ago, my daughter texted me and said she was having a hard time with the Bible Study topic her church group was studying. When I asked what the topic was, yes, it was on Revelation. At that moment, I knew that was what I was to do next. As I worked on the subject, I became so excited about the visions, the representations, and how it all began to take on a new, bright meaning to me, that it ended up as this publication.

Many people show little interest in reading Revelation, maybe because fear of not understanding the truth about judgment and end times. My prayer is that while you read this, it enhances your understanding and brings brightness to reading about the future and the present and helps "Unlock the Book of REVELATION."

Patti Hanni

Author's Note

According to the **Encyclopedia Britannica Online**, *Revelation to John*, also called ***Book of Revelation*** or ***Apocalypse of John***, the last book of the **New Testament, "*Revelation to John*** appears to be a collection of separate units composed by unknown authors who lived during the last quarter of the 1st century, though it purports to have been written by an individual named John—who calls himself "the servant" of Jesus—at Patmos, in the Aegean Sea. The text includes no indication that John of Patmos and St. John the Apostle are the same person."

Each chapter of this study guide correlates to the same numbered chapter in the Book of Revelation. The intention is that the reader will read the Biblical chapter as they are reading this guide.

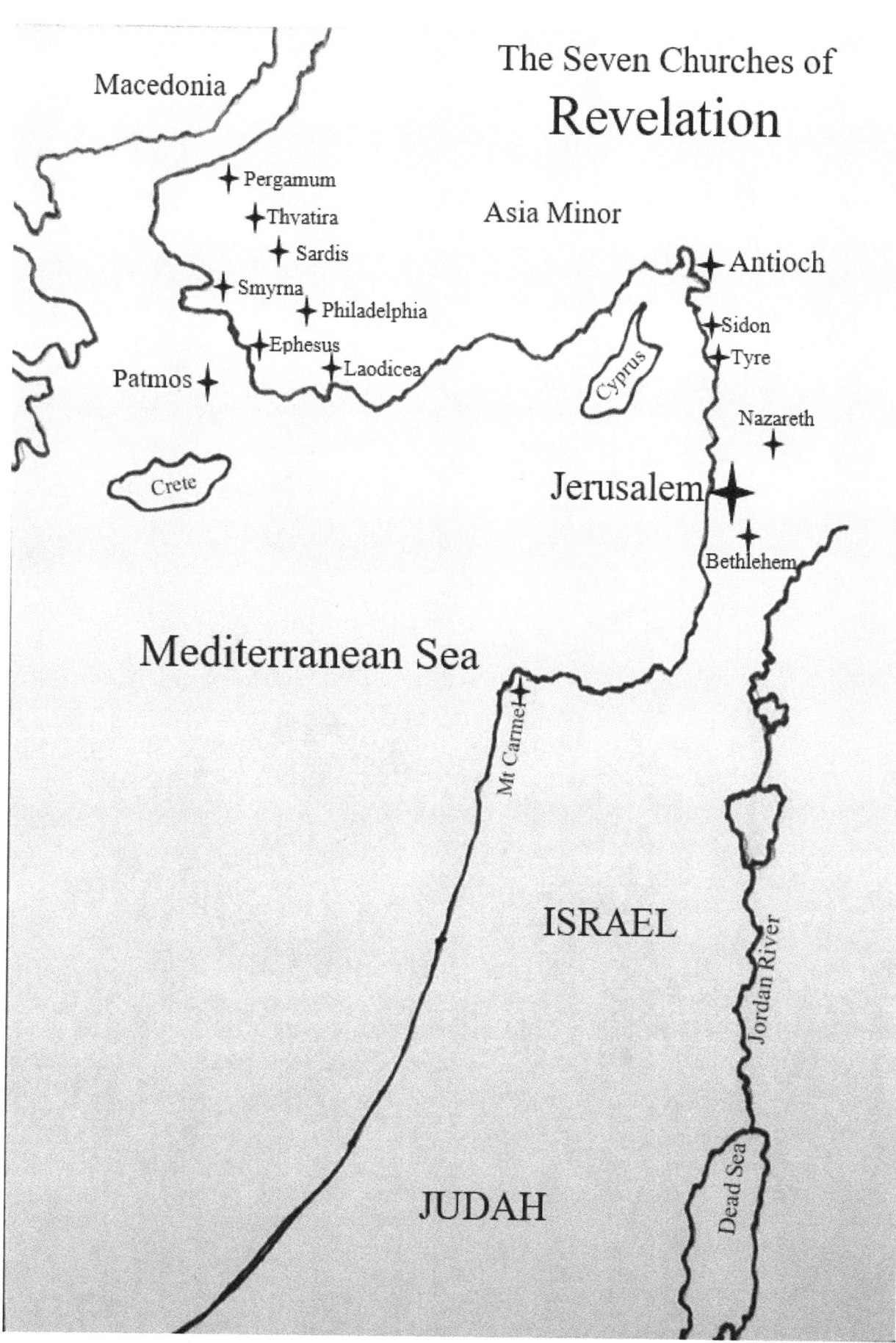

The Seven Seals of Revelation

1st Seal	2nd Seal	3rd Seal	4th Seal	5th Seal	6th Seal	7th Seal
White Horse: GOSPEL Revelation 6:1-2	Red Horse: **WAR** Revelation 6:3-4	Black Horse: FAMINE Revelation 6:5-6	Pale Horse: Pestilence Revelation 6:7-8	Martyrdom & Great Tribulation Revelation 6:9-11	Preview of the Wrath Of God Revelation 6:12-17	Seven Trumpet Plagues Revelation 8:2

Silence in Heaven Revelation 8:1-6

Seven Trumpets: The Day of the Lord

1st Trumpet	2nd Trumpet	3rd Trumpet	4th Trumpet	5th Trumpet	6th Trumpet	7th Trumpet
Green grass and 1/3 of the trees are burned up Revelation 8:7	1/3 of sea becomes blood; Fire destroys 1/3 of ships and sea life Revelation 8:8-9	1/3 of waters turn bitter Revelation 8:10-11	1/3 of sun, moon and stars do not shine Revelation 8:12	"Locusts" wield the Beast's military power. Revelation 9:1-12	200 million-man army gathers Revelation 9:13-21	The Kingdom is proclaimed. 2nd Coming Revelation 11:15-19

Seven Last Plagues

1st Plague	2nd Plague	3rd Plague	4th Plague	5th Plague	6th Plague	7th Plague
Sores afflict those who accepted the mark of the Beast Revelation 16:2	Sea turns to blood; all sea creatures die Revelation 16:3	Rivers turn to blood Revelation 16:4-7	Mankind scorched by the Sun, blasphemes God. Revelation 16:8-9	The Beast's seat of government is afflicted Revelation 16:10-11	The Euphrates is dried up; world armies gather to Armageddon. Revelation 16:12-16	The earth is utterly shaken Revelation 16:17-21

REVELATION

INTRODUCTION

Near the end of his life, John received a vision from Christ, which he recorded for the benefit of the seven churches in Asia and for Christians throughout history. This is the only book in the Bible that promises a blessing to those who listen to its words and do what it says.

Revelation is a book about the future and about the present. It offers future hope to all believers, especially those who have suffered for their faith, by proclaiming Christ's final victory over evil and the reality of eternal life with Him. It also gives present guidance as it teaches us about Jesus Christ and how we should live for Him now. Through graphic pictures we learn that (1) Jesus Christ is coming again (2) evil will be judged, and (3) the dead will be raised to judgment resulting in eternal life or eternal destruction.

According to tradition, John, the author, was the only one of Jesus' original 12 disciples who was not killed for the faith. He also wrote the Gospel of John and the letters 1, 2, and 3 John. When he wrote Revelation, John was in exile on the island of Patmos in the Aegean Sea, sent there by the Romans for his witness about Jesus Christ. See his profile in John 13.

The Book of Revelation unveils Christ's full identity and God's plan for the end of the world, and it focuses on Jesus Christ, His second coming, His victory over evil, and the establishment of His Kingdom. As you read Revelation, do not focus so much on the timetable of events or the details of John's imagery that you miss the main message—the infinite love, power, and justice of the Lord Jesus Christ.

John was acquainted with Jewish apocalyptic works, but his book is different in several ways: (1) he uses his own name rather than the name of an ancient hero; (2) he denounces evil and exhorts people to high Christian standards; (3) he offers hope rather than gloom. When John says that "the time is near," he is urging readers to be ready at all times for the last judgment and the establishment of God's Kingdom. We do not know when these events will occur, but we must always be prepared. The events will happen quickly and there will not be a second chance to change sides.

CHAPTER 1
John's Greeting to the Seven Churches

The "Sevenfold Spirit" is another name for the Holy Spirit. The number seven is used throughout Revelation to symbolize completeness and perfection.

The Trinity—the Father ("the one who is, who was, and who is to come"), the Holy Spirit (the Sevenfold Spirit), and the Son (Jesus Christ)—is the source of all truth (John 14:6, 17; 1 John 2:27; Revelation 19:11). Thus, we can be assured that John's message is reliable and is God's word to us.

Many hesitate to witness about their faith in Christ because they do not feel the change in their lives has been spectacular enough. But you qualify as a witness for Jesus because of what He has done for you, not because of what you have done for Him. The fact that the all-powerful God has offered eternal life to you is nothing short of spectacular.

Jesus is portrayed as the all-powerful King, victorious in battle, glorious in peace. He is not just a humble Earthly teacher He is the glorious God.

The Christian church was facing severe persecution. Almost all believers were socially, politically, or economically suffering because of this empire-wide persecution, and some were even being killed for their faith. John was exiled to the island of Patmos because he refused to stop preaching the Good News.

The seven gold lampstands are the seven churches in Asia, and Jesus stands among them. No matter what the churches face, Jesus protects them with His all-encompassing love and reassuring power. The "Son of Man" is Jesus himself. The title Son of Man occurs many times in the New Testament in reference to Jesus as the Messiah.

The sword in Jesus' mouth symbolizes the power and force of His message. His words of judgment are as sharp as swords (Isaiah 49:2; Hebrews 4:12). Our sins have convicted and sentenced us, but Jesus holds the keys of death and the grave. He alone can free us from eternal bondage to Satan. He alone has the power and authority to set us free from sin's control.

Who are the "angels of the seven churches?" Some say they are angels designated to guard the churches, others say they are elders or pastors of the local churches. Because the letters in Chapters 2 and 3 contain reprimands, it is doubtful that these angels are heavenly messengers. If these are Earthly leaders or messengers, they are accountable to God for the churches they represent.

NOTES

CHAPTER 2
The Message to the Church of Ephesus

Ephesus was the capital of Asia Minor, a center of land and sea trade, and, along with Alexandria and Antioch in Syria, one of the three most influential cities in the eastern part of the Roman Empire. The Temple of Artemis, one of the ancient wonders of the world, was in this city, and a major industry was the manufacture of images of this goddess (Acts 19:21-41). Paul ministered in Ephesus for three years and warned the Ephesians that false teachers would come and try to draw people away from the faith (Acts 20:29-31). False teachers did indeed cause problems in the Ephesian church, but the church resisted them, as we can see from Paul's letter to the Ephesians.

The one who "walks among the seven gold lampstands" (the seven churches) is Jesus. He holds the "seven stars in high right hand" (the messengers of the churches), indicating His power and authority over the churches and their leaders. Ephesus had become a large, proud church, and Jesus' message would remind them that He alone is the head of the body of believers.

Does God care about your church? If you are tempted to doubt it, look more closely at these seven letters. The Lord of the Universe knew each of these churches and its precise situation. In each letter, Jesus told John to write about specific people, places, and events. He praised believers for their successes and told them how to correct their failures. Just as Jesus cared for each of these churches, He cares for yours. He wants it to reach it's greatest potential. The group of believers with whom you worship and serve is God's vehicle for changing the world. Take it seriously—God does.

Over a long period of time, the church in Ephesus had steadfastly refused to tolerate sin among its members. This was not easy in a city noted for immoral sexual practices associated with the worship of the goddess Artemis. We also are living in times of widespread sin and sexual immorality. It is popular to be open-minded toward many types of sin, calling them personal choices or alternative lifestyles. But when the body of believers begins to tolerate sin in the church, it is lowering the standards and compromising the church's witness. Remember that God's approval is infinitely more important than the world's.

Christ commended the church at Ephesus for 1) working hard, 2) patiently enduring, 3) not tolerating evil people, 4) critically examining the claims of false apostles, and 5) suffering without quitting. Every church should have these characteristics. But these good efforts should spring from our love for Jesus Christ. Both Jesus and John stressed love for one another as an authentic proof of the Good News (John 13:34; 1 John 3:18-19). In the battle to maintain sound teaching and moral and doctrinal purity, it is possible to lose a charitable spirit. Prolonged conflict can weaken or destroy our patience and affection. In defending the faith, guard against any structure or rigidity that weakens love. Do not lose your first love!

Paul had once commended the church at Ephesus for its love for God and others (Ephesians 1:15), but many of the church founders had died and many of the second-generation believers had lost their zeal for God. They were a busy church—the members did much to benefit themselves and the community—but they were acting out of the wrong motives. Work for God must be motivated by love for God or it will not last.

Just as when a man and woman fall in love, so also new believers rejoice at their newfound forgiveness. But when we lose sight of the seriousness of sin, we begin to lose the thrill of our forgiveness (2 Peter 1:9). In the first steps of your Christian life, you may have had enthusiasm without knowledge. Do you now have knowledge without enthusiasm? Both are necessary if we are to keep love for God intense and untarnished (Hebrews 10:32-35). Do you love God with the same fervor as when you were a new Christian?

For Jesus to "remove your lampstand from its place" would mean the church would cease to be an effective church. Just as the seven-branched candlestick in the Temple gave light for the priests to see, the churches were to give light to their surrounding communities. But Jesus warned them that their lights could go out. In fact, Jesus himself would extinguish any light that did not fulfill its purpose. The church needed to repent of its sins.

The Nicolaitans were believers who compromised their faith to enjoy some of the sinful practices of Ephesian society. The name Nicolaitans is held by some to be roughly the Greek equivalent of the Hebrew word for "Balaamites." Balaam was a prophet who induced the Israelites to carry out their lustful desires. When we want to take part in an activity that we know is wrong, we may make excuses to justify our behavior, saying that it is not as bad as it seems or that it will not hurt our faith. Christ has strong words for those who look for excuses to sin.

Through John, Jesus commended the church at Ephesus for hating the wicked practices of the Nicolaitans. Note that they did not hate the people, just their sinful actions. We should accept and love all people and refuse to tolerate any evil. God cannot tolerate sin, and he expects us to stand against it. The world needs Christians who will stand for God's truth and point people toward right living.

We are victorious by believing in Christ, persevering, remaining faithful, and living as one who follows Christ. Such a life brings great rewards.

Two trees were in the Garden of Eden—the tree of life and the tree of knowledge of good and evil (Genesis 2:9). Eating from the tree of life brought eternal life with God, eating from the tree of knowledge brought realization of good and evil. When Adam and Eve ate from the tree of knowledge, they disobeyed God's command. So, they were excluded from Eden and barred from eating from the tree of life. Eventually evil will be destroyed and believers will be brought into a restored paradise. In the new Earth, everyone will eat from the Tree of life and live forever.

The Message to the Church in Smyrna

The city of Smyrna was about 25 miles north of Ephesus. It was nicknamed "Port of Asia" because it had an excellent harbor on the Aegean Sea. The church in this city shrugged against two hostile forces; a Jewish population strongly opposed to Christianity, and a non-Jewish population that was loyal to Rome and supported emperor worship. Persecution and suffering were inevitable in an environment like this.

Persecution comes from Satan, not from God. Satan will cause believers to be thrown into prison and even killed. But believers need not fear death, because it will only result in their receiving the crown of life. Satan may harm their Earthly bodies, but he can do them no spiritual harm. The "synagogue of Satan" means that these Jews were serving Satan's purposes, not God's, when they gathered to worship. "Ten days" means that although persecution would be intense, it would be relatively short. It would have a definite beginning and end, and God would remain in complete control.

Pain is part of life, but it is never easy to suffer, no matter what the cause. Jesus commended the church at Smyrna for its faith in suffering. He then encouraged the believers that they need not fear the future if they remained faithful. If you are experiencing difficult times, do not let them turn you away from God. Instead, let them draw you toward greater faithfulness. Trust God and remember your heavenly reward.

Smyrna was famous for its athletic games. A crown was the victory wreath, the trophy for the champion at the games. If we have been faithful, we will receive the prize of victory—eternal life (James 1:12). The message to the Smyrna church was to remain faithful during suffering because God is in control and His promises are reliable. Jesus never says that by being faithful to Him we will avoid troubles, suffering and persecution. Rather, we must be faithful to Him in our sufferings. Only then will our faith prove to be genuine. We remain faithful by keeping our eyes on Christ and on what He promises us now, and in the future (Philippians 3:13-14; 2 Timothy 4:8).

Believers and unbelievers alike experience physical death. All people will be resurrected, but believers will be resurrected to eternal life with God while unbelievers will be resurrected to be punished with a second death, eternal separation from God.

The city of Pergamum was built on a hill 1,000 feet above the surrounding countryside, creating a natural fortress. It was a sophisticated city, a center of Greek Culture and education, with a 200,000-volume library. But it was also the center of four cults, and it rivaled Ephesus in its worship of idols. The city's chief god was Asclepius, whose symbol was a serpent and who was considered the god of healing. People came to Pergamum from all over the world to seek healing from this god.

Just as the Romans used their swords for authority and judgment, Jesus' sharp two-edged sword represents God's ultimate authority and judgment. It may also represent God's future separation of believers from unbelievers. Unbelievers cannot experience the eternal rewards of living in God's Kingdom.

As the center for four idolatrous cults (Zeus, Dionysius, Asclepius, and Athene), Pergamum was called the city "where the great throne of Satan is located.) Surrounded by worship of Satan and the Roman emperor as god, the church at Pergamum refused to renounce its faith, even when Satan's worshipers martyred one of its members. Standing firm against the strong pressures and temptations of society is never easy but the alternative is deadly.

It was not easy to be a Christian in Pergamum. Believers experienced great pressure to compromise or leave the faith. Nothing is known about Antipas except that he did not compromise. He was faithful, and he died for his faith. Apparently, however, some in the church were tolerating those who taught or practiced what Christ opposed. Compromise can be defined as a blending of the qualities of two different things or a concession of principles. Cooperate with people as much as you can, but avoid any alliance, partnership, or participation that could lead to immoral practice.

There is room for differences of opinions among Christians in some areas, but there is no room for heresy and moral impurity. Your town might not participate in idol feasts, but it probably has pornography, sexual sin, cheating, gossiping, and lying. Do not tolerate sin by bowing to the pressure to be open-minded.

Balak was a king who feared the large number of Israelites traveling through his country, so he hired Balaam to pronounce a curse on them. Balaam refused at first, but an offer of money changed his mind (Numbers chapters 22-24). Later Balaam influenced the Israelites to turn to idol worship (Numbers 31:16; 2 Peter 2:15; Jude 1:11). Here Christ rebuked the church for tolerating those who, like Balaam, lead people away from God. The sword is God's judgment against rebellious nations (Chapter 19:15 and 21) and all forms of sin.

This "manna that has been hidden away in heaven" suggests the spiritual nourishment that the faithful believers will receive. As the Israelites traveled toward the Promised Land, God provided manna from heaven for their physical nourishment (Exodus 16:13-18). Jesus, as the bread of life (John 6:51), provides spiritual nourishment that satisfies our deepest hunger.

It is unclear what the white stones are or exactly what the name on each will be. Because they relate to the hidden manna, they may be symbols of the believer's eternal nourishment or eternal life. The stones are significant because each will bear the new name of every person who genuinely believes in Christ. They are the evidence that a person has been accepted by God and declared worthy to receive eternal life. A person's name represented his or her character. God will give us a new name and a new heart.

The Message to the Church in Thyatira

Thyatira was a working person's town, with many trade guilds for cloth making, dyeing, and pottery. Lydia, Paul's first convert in

Philippi, was a merchant from Thyatira (Acts 16:14). The city was basically secular, with no focus on any religion.

The believers in Thyatira were commended for growing in good deeds. We should not only take comfort in gathering for worship or rejoice when people give their lives to Christ in our church. We should also seek to grow in love, faith, and acts of service. Because the times are critical, we must spend our days wisely and faithfully.

A woman in the church in Thyatira was teaching that immorality was not a serious matter for believers. Her name may have been Jezebel, or John may have used the name Jezebel to symbolize the kind of evil she was promoting. Jezebel, a pagan queen of Israel, was considered the most evil woman who ever lived (1 Kings chapters 19:1-2; 21:1-5; 2 Kings 9:7-10, 30-37, and her profile in 1 Kings 21).

Why is sexual immorality serious? Sex outside marriage always hurts someone. It hurts God because it shows that we prefer to satisfy our desires our own way instead of according to God's Word or to satisfy them immediately instead of waiting for His timing. It hurts others because it violates the commitment so necessary to a relationship. It hurts us because it often brings disease to our bodies and adversely affects our personalities. Sexual immorality has tremendous power to destroy families, churches, and communities because it destroys the integrity on which these relationships are built. God wants to protect us from hurting ourselves and others, thus, we are to have no part in sexual immorality, even if our culture accepts it.

In pagan temples, meat was often offered to idols. Then the meat that was not burned was sold to shoppers in the temple marketplace. Eating meat offered to idols was not wrong in itself, but it could violate the conscience of weaker Christian brothers and sisters who would be bothered by it (1 Corinthians 9 and Romans 14:2). Jezebel was obviously more concerned about her own selfish pleasures and freedom than about the needs and concerns of fellow believers.

Jezebel was unwilling to repent. Repent means "to change one's mind and to turn from sin" and its disastrous consequences to God and eternal life. In His mercy, God has given us time to decide to follow Him. Only our stubborn willfulness stands in the way.

We cannot hide from Christ; He knows what is in our heart and mind, and still He loves us. The sins we try to hide from God need to be confessed to Him.

The "deeper truths" of Satan were either false teaching advocated by heretics, or secret insights by so-called believers "guaranteed" to promote deeper spiritual life. We should hold tightly to the basics of our Christian faith and view with caution and counsel any new teaching that turns us away from the Bible, the fellowship of our church, or our basic confession of faith.

Christ says that those who overcome (those who remain faithful until the end and continue to please God) will rule over Christ's enemies and reign with Him as He judges evil (Psalm 2:8-9; Isaiah 30:14; Jeremiah 19:11; 1 Corinthians 6:2-3; Revelation 12:5; 19:15; 20:3-4).

Christ is also called the morning star in Chapter 22:16. A morning star appears just before dawn, when the night is coldest and darkest. When the world is at it bleakest point, Christ will burst onto the scene, exposing evil with His light of truth, and bringing His promised reward.

NOTES

CHAPTER 3
The Message to the Church in Sardis

The wealthy city of Sardis was in two locations. The older section of the city was on a mountain, and when its population outgrew the spot, a newer section was built in the valley below.

The "Sevenfold Spirit" is another name for the Holy Spirit. The seven stars are the messengers, or leaders, of the churches.

The problem in the Sardis church was not heresy but spiritual death. Despite its reputation for being active, Sardis was infested with sin, its deeds were evil, and its clothes soiled. The Spirit has no words of commendation for this church that looked so good on the outside but was so corrupt on the inside.

The church at Sardis was urged to obey the Christian truth they had heard when they first believed in Christ, to get back to the basics of the faith. It is important to grow in our knowledge of the Lord, to deepen our understanding through careful study. But no matter how much we learn; we must never abandon the basic truths about Jesus. Jesus will always be God's Son, and His sacrifice for our sins is permanent. No new truth from God will ever contradict these fundamental biblical teachings.

To be "clothed in white" means to be set apart for God and made pure. Christ promises future honor and eternal life to those who stand firm in their faith. The names of all believers are registered in the Book of Life. This book symbolizes God's knowledge of who belongs to Him. All such people are guaranteed a listing in the Book of Life and are introduced to the hosts of heaven as belonging to Christ (Luke 12:8-9).

The Message to the Church in Philadelphia

Philadelphia was founded by the citizens of Pergamum. The community was built in a frontier area as a gateway to the central plateau of Asia Minor. Philadelphia's residents kept barbarians out of the region and brought in Greek culture and language. The city was destroyed by an Earthquake in A.D. 17, and aftershocks kept the people so worried that most of them lived outside the city limits.

The "key of David" represents Christ's authority to open the door into His future Kingdom. After the door is opened, no one can close it—salvation is assured. Once it is closed, no one can open it—judgment is certain.

Some believe that "I will protect you from the great time of testing" means there will be a future time of great tribulation from which true believers will be spared. Others interpret this to mean that the church will go through the time of tribulation and that God will keep them strong during it. Still others believe this refers to times of great distress in general, the church's suffering through the ages. Whatever the case, our emphasis should be on patiently obeying God no matter what we may face.

Christians have differing gifts, abilities, experience, and maturity. God does not expect us all to be and act the same, but He does expect us to "hold on" to what we have, to persevere in using our resources for Him. The Philadelphians are commended for their efforts to obey (Chapter 3:8) and encouraged to hold tightly to whatever strength they have. You may be a new believer and feel that your faith and spiritual strength are little. Use what you have to live for Christ, and God will commend you.

The new Jerusalem is the future dwelling of the people of God (2:12). We will have a new citizenship in God's future Kingdom. Everything will be new, pure, and secure.

The Message to the Church in Laodicea

Laodicea was the wealthiest of the seven cities, known for its banking industry, manufacture of wool, and a medical school that produced eye ointment. But the city had always had a problem with its water supply. At one time an aqueduct was built to bring water to the city from hot springs. But by the time the water reached the city, it was neither hot nor refreshingly cool—only lukewarm. The church had become as bland as the tepid water that came into the city.

Lukewarm water makes a disgusting drink. The church in Laodicea had become lukewarm and thus distasteful and repugnant. The believers did not take a stand for anything, indifference had led to idleness. By neglecting to do anything for Christ, the church had become hardened and self-satisfied, and it was destroying itself. There is nothing more disgusting than a half-hearted, nominal Christian who is self-sufficient. Do not settle for following God halfway. Let Christ fire up your faith and get you into action.

Some believers assume that numerous material possessions are a sign of God's spiritual blessing. Laodicea was a wealthy city, and the church was also wealthy. But what the Laodiceans could see and buy had become more valuable to them than what is unseen and eternal. Wealth, luxury, and ease can make people feel confident, satisfied, and complacent. But no matter how much you possess or how much money you make, you have nothing if you do not have a vital relationship with Christ.

How does your current level of wealth affect your spiritual desire? Instead of centering your life primarily on comfort and luxury, find your true riches in Christ.

Laodicea was known for its great wealth; Christ told the Laodiceans to buy their gold from Him (real spiritual treasures). The city was proud of its cloth and dyeing industries; Christ told them to purchase white garments from Him (His righteousness). Laodicea prided itself on its precious eye ointment that healed many eye problems. Christ told them to get medicine from Him to heal their eyes so they could see the truth (John 9:39). Christ was showing the Laodiceans that true value was not in material possessions but in a right relationship with God. Their possessions and achievements were valueless compared with the everlasting future of Christ's Kingdom.

God would discipline this lukewarm church unless it turned from its indifference toward Him. God's purpose in discipline is not to punish but to bring people back to Him. Are you lukewarm in your devotion to God? God may discipline you to help you out of your uncaring attitude, but he uses only loving discipline. You can avoid God's discipline by drawing near to him again through confession, service, worship, and studying His Word. Just as the spark of love can be rekindled in marriage, so the Holy Spirit can reignite our zeal for God when we allow Him to work in our heart.

The Laodicean church was complacent and rich. They felt self-satisfied, but they did not have Christ's presence among them. Christ knocked at the door of their hearts, but they were so busy enjoying worldly pleasures that they did not notice that He was trying to enter. The pleasures of this world—money, security, material possessions—can be dangerous because their temporary satisfaction makes us indifferent to God's offer of lasting satisfaction. If you find yourself feeling indifferent to church, to God, or to the Bible, you have begun to shut God out of your life. Leave the door of your heart constantly open to God and you will not need to worry about hearing His knock. Letting Him in is your only hope for lasting fulfillment.

Jesus knocks at the door of our heart because He wants to save us and have fellowship with us. He is patient and persistent in trying to get through to us—not breaking and entering but knocking. He allows us to decide whether or not to open our life to Him. Do you intentionally keep His life-changing presence and power on the other side of the door?

At the end of each letter to these churches, the believers were urged to listen and understand what was written to them. Although a different message was addressed to each church, all the messages contain warnings and principles for everyone. Which letter speaks most directly to your church? Which has the greatest bearing on your own spiritual condition currently? How will you respond?

NOTES

CHAPTER 4
Message for the Church

Moving from the conditions within the churches in Asia to the future of the universal church, John sees the course of coming events in a way similar to Daniel and Ezekiel. Many of these passages contain clear spiritual teachings, but others seem beyond our ability to understand. The clear teaching of this book is that God will defeat all evil in the end. We must live in obedience to Jesus Christ, the coming Conqueror and Judge.

Worshipping God in Heaven

Chapters 4 and 5 record glimpses into Christ's glory. Here we see into the throne room of heaven. God is on the throne and orchestrating all the events that John will record. The world is not spinning out of control; the God of Creation will carry out His plans as Christ initiates the final battle with the forces of evil. John shows us heaven before showing us Earth so that we will not be frightened by future events.

The voice John had first heard that sounded like a trumpet blast was the voice of Christ.

Four times in the book of Revelation John says he was "in the Spirit". This expression means that the Holy Spirit was giving him a vision—showing him situations and events he could not have seen with mere human eyesight. All true prophecy comes from God through the Holy Spirit (2 Peter 1:20,21).

Who are these 24 elders? Because there were 12 tribes of Israel in the Old Testament and 12 apostles in the New Testament, the 24 elders in this vision probably represent all the redeemed of God for all time (both before and after Christ's death and resurrection). They symbolize all those—both Jews and Gentiles—who are now part of God's family. The 24 elders show us that all the redeemed of the Lord are worshiping Him.

In Revelation, lightning and thunder relate to significant events in heaven. They remind us of the lightning at Mount Sinai when God gave the people His laws (Exodus 19:16). The Old Testament often uses such imagery to reflect God's power and majesty (Psalm 77:18).

The "Seven Spirits" is another name for the Holy Spirit. See also Zechariah 4:2-6, where the seven lamps are equated with the one Spirit.

Glass was rare in New Testament times, and crystal-clear glass was virtually impossible to find (see 1 Corinthians 13:120). The "sea of glass" highlights both the magnificence and holiness of God.

Just as the Holy Spirit is seen symbolically in the seven lighted lamps, so the "four living beings" represent the attributes (the qualities and character) of God. These creatures were not real animals. Like the cherubim (the highest order of the angels) they guard God's throne, lead others in worship, and proclaim God's holiness. God's attributes symbolized in the animal-like appearance of these creatures are majesty and power (the lion), faithfulness (the ox), intelligence (the human), and sovereignty (the eagle). The Old Testament prophet Ezekiel saw four similar creatures in one of his visions (Ezekiel 1:5-10).

The point of this chapter is summed up in verse 11. All the creatures in heaven and Earth will praise and honor God because He is the creator and sustainer of everything.

NOTES

CHAPTER 5
The Lamb Opens the Scroll

Chapter 5 continues the glimpse into heaven begun in Chapter 4. In John's day, books were written on scrolls—pieces of papyrus or vellum up to 30 feet long, rolled up and sealed with clay or wax. The scroll that John sees contains the full account of what God has in store for the world. The seven seals indicate the importance of its contents (see chart at beginning of study). The seals are located throughout the scroll so that as each one is broken, more of the scroll can be read to reveal another phase of God's plan for the end of the world. Only Christ is worthy to break the seals and open the scroll (v. 3-5).

The Lion, Jesus, proved Himself worthy to break the seals and open the scroll by living a perfect life of obedience to God, dying on the cross for the sins of the world, and rising from the dead to show His power and authority over evil and death. Only Christ conquered sin, death, hell, and Satan himself; so only He can be trusted with the world's future. "Heir to David's throne" refers to Jesus being from David's family line, thus fulfilling the promise of the Messiah in the Old Testament.

Jesus Christ is pictured as both a Lion (symbolizing His authority and power) and a Lamb (symbolizing His submission to God's will). One of the elders calls John to look at the Lion. But when John looks, he sees a Lamb. Christ the Lamb was the perfect sacrifice for the sins of all, therefore, only He can save us from the terrible events revealed by the scroll. Christ the Lamb won the greatest battle of all. He defeated all the forces of evil by dying on the cross. The role of Christ the Lion will be to lead the battle where Satan is finally defeated. Christ the Lion is victorious because of what Christ the Lamb has already done. We will participate in his victory, not because of our effort or goodness, but because He has promised eternal life to all who believe in Him.

John says the Lamb "has been killed;" the wounds inflicted on Jesus' body during His trial and crucifixion could still be seen (John 20:24-31). Jesus was called the Lamb of God by John the Baptist. In the Old Testament, lambs were sacrificed to atone for sins; the Lamb of God died as the final sacrifice for all sins (Isaiah 53:7; Hebrews 10:1-12, 18).

The horns symbolize strength and power (1 Kings 22:11: and Zechariah 1:18). Although Christ is a sacrificial lamb, He is in no way weak. He was killed, but now He lives in God's strength and power. In Zechariah 4:2-20, the eyes are equated with the seven lamps and the one Spirit.

People from every nation are praising God before His throne. God's message of salvation and eternal life is not limited to a specific culture, race, or country. Anyone who comes to God in repentance and faith is accepted by Him and will be part of His Kingdom. Do not allow prejudice or bias to keep you from sharing Christ with others. Christ welcomes all people into His Kingdom.

The son of God's people praises Christ's work. He 1) was killed, 2) ransomed them with His blood, 3) gathered them into a Kingdom, 4) made them priests, and 5) appointed them to reign on the Earth. Jesus has already died and paid the penalty for sin. He is now gathering us into His Kingdom and making us priests. In the future we will reign with Him. Worship God and praise Him for what He has done, what He is doing, and what He will do for all who trust in

Him. When we realize the glorious future that awaits us, we will find the strength to face our present difficulties.

The believers' song praises Christ for bringing them into the Kingdom and making them kings and priests. While now we are sometimes despised and mocked for our faith (John 15:17-27), in the future we will reign over all the Earth (Luke 22:29-30). Christ's death made all believers priests of God—the channels of blessing between God and people (1 Peter 2:5-9).

Angels are spiritual beings created by God who help carry out His work on Earth. They bring messages (Luke 1:26-28, protect God's people (Daniel 6:22), offer encouragement (Genesis 16:7), give guidance (Exodus 14:19), bring punishment (2 Samuel 24:16), patrol the Earth (Ezekiel 1:9-14), and fight the forces of evil (2 Kings 6:16-18, Revelation 20:1). There are both good and evil angels, but because evil angels are allied with Satan, they have considerably less power and authority than good angels. Eventually, the main role of the good angels will be to offer continuous praise to God.

The scene in chapter 5 shows us that only the Lamb, Jesus Christ, is worthy to open the scroll (the events of history). Jesus, not Satan, holds the future. Jesus Christ is in control, and He alone is worthy to set into motion the events of the last days of history.

NOTES

CHAPTER 6
Opening the Seven Seals

The Lamb Breaks the First Six Seals

This is the first of three seven-part judgements (See chart at beginning of study). The trumpets (chapters 8-9) and the bowls (chapter 16) are the other two. As each seal is opened, Christ the Lamb sets in motion events that will bring about the end of human history. This scroll is not completely opened until the seventh seal is broken (8:1). The contents of the scroll reveal humankind's depravity and portray God's authority over the events of human history.

Four horses appear as the first four seals are opened. The horses represent God's judgment of people's sin and rebellion. God is directing human history—even using His enemies to accomplish His purposes. The four horses are a foretaste of the final judgments yet to come. Some view this chapter as a parallel to the Olivet Discourse (Matthew 24). The imagery of four horses is also found in Zechariah 6:1-8.

Each of the four horses is a different color. Some assume that the white horse represents victory and that its rider must be Christ (because Christ later rides to victory on a white horse)—(Ch19:11). But because the other three horses relate to judgment and destruction, this rider on a white horse would most likely not be Christ, he is referred to as the conqueror (some say the Antichrist). The four are part of the unfolding judgment of God, and it would be premature for Christ to ride forth as conqueror. The other horses represent different kinds of judgment, red for warfare and bloodshed; black for famine; pale green for death. The high prices of wheat and barley illustrate famine conditions. But the worst is yet to come. It is not clear whether "the Grave" was on a separate horse than Death or merely rode along with Death, but the riders described in verses 2-8 are commonly referred to the four horsemen of the Apocalypse.

The four riders are given power over one-fourth of the Earth, indicating that God is still limiting His judgment—it is not yet complete. With these judgments there is still time for unbelievers to turn to Christ and away from their sin, in this case, the limited punishment not only demonstrates God's wrath on sin but also His merciful love in giving people yet another opportunity to turn to Him before He brings final judgment.

The altar represents the altar of sacrifice in the Temple where animals were sacrificed to atone for sins. Instead of the animals' blood at the base of the altar, John saw the souls of martyrs who had died for preaching the Good News. These martyrs were told that still more would lose their lives for their belief in Christ (Chapter 6:11). In the face of warfare, famine, persecution, and death, Christians will be called on to stand firmly for what they believe. Only those who endure to the end will be rewarded by God (Mark 13:13).

The martyrs are eager for God to bring justice to the Earth, but they are told to wait. God is not waiting until a certain number is reached, but He is promising that those who suffer and die for their faith will not be forgotten. Rather, they will be singled out by God for special honor. We may wish for justice immediately as these martyrs did, but we must be patient. God works according to His own timetable, and He promises justice. No suffering for the sake of God's Kingdom, however, is wasted.

The sixth seal changes the scene back to the physical world. The first five judgments were directed toward specific areas, but His judgment is universal. Everyone will be afraid when the Earth itself trembles.

At the sight of God sitting on the throne, all human beings, great and small, will be terrified, calling for the mountains to fall on them so that they will not have to face the judgment of the Lamb. This vivid picture was not intended to frighten believers. For them, the Lamb is a gentle Savior. But to those kings, rulers, and generals and other powerful people who previously showed no fear of God and arrogantly flaunted their unbelief will find that they were wrong, and in that day they will have to face God's wrath, but those who belong to Christ will receive a reward rather than punishment. Do you belong to Christ? If so, you need not fear these final days.

NOTES

CHAPTER 7
God's People Will Be Preserved

The sixth seal has been opened and the people of the Earth have tried to hide from God, saying "Who will be able to survive?" (Chapter 6:12-17). Just when all hope seems lost, four angels hold back the four winds of judgment until God's people are sealed as His own. Only then will God open the seventh seal (Chapter 8:1).

A seal on a scroll or document identified and protected its contents. God places His own seal on His followers, identifying them as His own and guaranteeing His protection over their souls. This shows how valuable we are to Him. Our physical bodies may be beaten, maimed, or even destroyed, but nothing can harm our souls when we have been sealed by God, (Ephesians 1:13).

God's seal is placed on the foreheads of His servants. The seal is the exact opposite of the mark of the beast explained in Chapter 13:16. These two marks place the people in two distinct categories—those owned by God and those owned by Satan.

The number 144,000 is 12x12x1,000, symbolizing completeness—all God's followers will be brought safely to Him; not one will be overlooked or forgotten. God seals these believers either by withdrawing them from the Earth (this is called the Rapture) or by giving them special strength and courage to make it through this time of great persecution, the seal does not necessarily guarantee protection from physical harm—many will die (6:11)—but God will protect them from spiritual harm. No matter what happens. They will be brought to their reward of eternal life. Their destiny is secure. These believers will not fall away from God even though they may undergo intense persecution. This is not saying that 144,000 individuals must be sealed before the persecution comes, but that when persecution begins, the faithful will have already been sealed (marked by God), and they will remain true to Him until the end.

This is a different list from the usual listing of the 12 tribes in the Old Testament, because it is a symbolic list of God's true followers. 1) Judah is mentioned first because Judah is both the tribe of David and of Jesus the Messiah, (Genesis 49:8-12; Matthew 1:1). 2) Levi had no tribal allotment because of the Levites' work for God in the Temple (Deuteronomy 18:1), but here the tribe is given a place as a reward for faithfulness. 3) Dan is not mentioned because it was known for rebellion and idolatry, traits unacceptable for God's followers (Genesis 49:17). 4) The two tribes representing Joseph (usually called Ephraim and Manasseh, after Joseph's sons) are here called Joseph and Manasseh because of Ephraim's rebellion. Genesis 49 explains the story of the beginning of these 12 tribes.

Praise From the Great Multitude

Who is this vast crowd? While some interpreters identify it as the martyrs described in 6:9, it may also be the same group as the 144,000 just mentioned (7:4-8). The 144,000 were sealed by God before the great time of persecution; the vast crowd was brought to eternal life, as God had promised. Before, they were being prepared, now, they are victorious. This crowd in heaven is composed of all those who remained faithful to God throughout the generations. No true believer ever need worry about which group he or she will be in. God includes and protects each of us, and we are guaranteed a place in His presence.

People try many methods to remove the guilt of sin—good deeds, intellectual pursuits, and even casting blame on others. The crown in heaven however, praises God, saying that salvation comes from Him and from the Lamb. Salvation from sin's penalty can come only through Jesus Christ. Have you had the guilt of sin removed in the only way possible?

"The great tribulation" has been explained in several ways. Some believe it refers to the suffering of believers through the ages; others believe that there is a specific time of intense tribulation yet to come. In either case, these believers come through their times of suffering by remaining loyal to God. Because they remain faithful, God will give them eternal life with Him. (7:17).

It is difficult to imagine how blood could make any cloth white, but the blood of Jesus Christ is the world's greatest purifier because it removes the stain of sin. White symbolizes sinless perfection or holiness, which can be given to people only by the death of the sinless Lamb of God on our behalf. This is a picture of how we are saved through faith (Isaiah 1:18; Romans 3:21-26).

God will provide for His children's needs in their eternal home where there will be no hunger, thirst, or pain, and He will wipe away all tears. When you are suffering or torn apart by sorrow, take comfort in this promise of complete protection and relief.

In verses 1-8 we see the believers receiving a seal to protect them through a time of great tribulation and suffering, in verses 9-17 we see the believers finally with God in heaven. All who have been faithful through the ages are singing before God's throne. Their tribulations and sorrows are over; no more tears for sin, for all sins are forgiven, no more tears for suffering, for all suffering is over; no more tears for death, for all believers have been resurrected to die no more.

NOTES

CHAPTER 8
The Lamb Breaks the Seventh Seal

When the seventh seal is opened, the seven trumpet judgments are revealed. In the same way, the seventh trumpet will announce the seven bowl judgments (in Chapter 11 and chapter 16). The trumpet judgments, like the seal judgments, are only partial. God's final and complete judgment has not yet come. An incense burner filled with live coals was used in Temple worship. Incense was poured on the coals, and the sweet-smelling smoke drifted upward, symbolizing believers' prayers ascending to God (Exodus 30:7-9).

The trumpet blasts have three purposes: 1) to warn that judgment is certain, 2) to call the forces of good and evil to battle, and 3) to announce the return of the King, the Messiah. These warnings urge us to make sure our faith is fixed on Christ. Since only one-third of the Earth is destroyed by these trumpet judgments, this is only a partial judgment from God. His full wrath is yet to be unleashed.

Habakkuk used the image of an eagle to symbolize swiftness and destruction (Habakkuk 1:6). The picture here is also of an eagle flying over all the Earth, warning of the terrors yet to come. While both believers and unbelievers experience the terrors described in verses 7-12, those "who belong to this world" are the unbelievers who will meet spiritual harm through the next three trumpet judgments. God has guaranteed believers protection from spiritual harm (Chapter 7:2-3).

In Chapter 6:10, the martyrs call out to God, "how long will it be before you judge the people who belong to this world for what they have done to us? When will you avenge our blood against these people?" As we see the world's wickedness, we, too, may cry out to God, "How long?" In the following chapters, the judgment comes at last. We may be distressed and impatient, but God has His plan and His timing, and we must learn to trust Him to know what is best. Judgment is coming—be sure of that. Thank God for the time He has given you to turn from sin. Use the available time to work to help others turn to Him. Have you done all you can with the time God has given you?

NOTES

CHAPTER 9
The Fifth Trumpet Brings the First Terror

It is not known whether this "star" that fell from the sky is Satan, a fallen angel, Christ, or a good angel. Most likely it is a good angel, because the key to the shaft of the bottomless pit is normally held by Christ (Chapter 1:17-18), and it was temporarily given to this other being from heaven (see also Chapter 20:1). This being, whoever he may be, is still under God's control and authority. The bottomless pit represents the place of the demons and of Satan, the king of demons (Chapter 9:11). Luke 8:31 is another reference to the bottomless pit.

The prophet Joel described a locust plague as a fore-shadowing of the "day of the LORD," meaning God's coming judgment (Joel 2:1-10). In the Old Testament, locusts were symbols of destruction because they destroyed vegetation. Here, however, they symbolize an invasion of demons called to torture people who do not believe in God. The limitations placed on the demons (they could only torment people for five months) show that they are under God's authority.

Most likely these locusts are demons—evil spirits ruled by Satan who tempt people to sin. They were not created by Satan, because God is the Creator of all, rather, they are fallen angels who joined Satan in his rebellion. God limits what they can do, they can do nothing without His permission. Their main purpose on Earth is to prevent, distort, or destroy people's relationship with God. Because they are corrupt and degenerate, their appearance reflects the distortion of their spirits. While it is important to recognize their evil activity so we can stay away from them, we must avoid any curiosity about or involvement with demonic forces or with the occult.

The locust-demons have a leader whose name in Hebrew and in Greek means "Destroyer." It may be a play on words by John to show that those who worshiped the great god Apollo worshiped only a demon.

The Sixth Trumpet Brings the Second Terror

The altar in the Temple had four projections, one at each corner, and these were called the horns of the altar (Exodus 27:2).

The word "angels" here, means fallen angels or demons. These four unidentified demons will be exceedingly evil and destructive. But note that they do not have the power to release themselves and do their evil work on Earth. Instead, they are held back by God and will be released at a specific time, doing only what He allows them to do.

Here one-third of all people are killed. In Chapter 6:7-8, one-fourth of all people were killed. Thus, over one-half of the people in the world will have been killed by God's great judgments. Even more would have been killed if God had not set limits on the destruction.

In John's day, this number of mounted troops in an army was inconceivable, but today there are countries and alliances that could easily amass these many soldiers. This huge army, led by the four demons, will be sent out to destroy one-third of the Earth's population. But the judgment is still not complete.

These people were so hard-hearted that even plagues did not drive them to God. People do not usually fall into immorality and evil suddenly—they slip into it a little bit at a time until, hardly realizing what has happened, they are irrevocably mired in their wicked ways. Any person who allows sin to take root in his or her life will end up in this predicament. Temptation entertained today becomes sin tomorrow, a habit the next day, then death and separation from God forever (James 1:15). To think you could never become this evil is the first step toward a hard heart. Acknowledge you need to confess your sin before God.

NOTES

CHAPTER 10
The Angel and the Small Scroll

The purpose of this mighty angel is clear—to announce the final judgments on the Earth. His right foot on the sea and left foot on the land (Chapter 10:2) indicate that his words deal with all creation, not just a limited part as did the seal and trumpet judgments. The seventh trumpet (Chapter 11:15) will usher in the seven bowl judgments, which bring an end to the present world. When the universal judgment comes, God's truth will prevail.

We see two scrolls in Revelation. The first contains a revelation of judgments against evil (Chapter 5:1). The contents of the second small scroll are not indicated, but it also may contain a revelation of judgment.

Throughout history people have wanted to know what would happen in the future, and God reveals some of it in this book. But John was stopped from revealing certain parts of his vision. An angel also told the prophet Daniel that some visions he saw were not to be revealed yet to everyone (Daniel 12:9), and Jesus told his disciples that the time of the end is known by no one but God (Mark 13:32-33). God has revealed all we need to know to live for Him now. In our desire to be ready for the end, we must not place more emphasis on speculation about the last days than on living for God while we wait. When God's plan for human history is completely revealed, all prophecy will be fulfilled. The end of the age will have arrived (Chapter 11:15 and Ephesians 1:9-10).

The prophet Ezekiel had a vision in which he was told to eat a scroll filled with judgments against the nation of Israel (Ezekiel 3:1). The taste was sweet in his mouth, but the scroll's contents brought destruction—just like the scroll John was told to eat. God's Word is sweet to us as believers because it brings encouragement, but it sours our stomach because of the coming judgment we must pronounce on unbelievers.

NOTES

CHAPTER 11
The Two Witnesses

This Temple is most likely a symbol of the church (all true believers) because there will be no Temple in the new Jerusalem (Chapters 21 and 22). John measured the Temple to show that God is building walls of protection around His people to spare them from spiritual harm, and that there is a place reserved for all believers who remain faithful to God.

Those worshiping inside the Temple will be protected spiritually, but those outside will face great suffering. This is a way of saying that true believers will be protected through persecution, but those who refuse to believe will be destroyed. These two witnesses bear strong resemblance to Moses and Elijah, two of God's mighty prophets. With God's power, Moses called plagues down upon the nation of Egypt (Exodus Chapters 7-11). Elijah defeated the prophets of Baal (1 Kings 18). Both men appeared with Christ at His transfiguration (Matthew 17:1-7).

In the book of Revelation, numbers are likely to have symbolic rather than literal meanings. The 42 months or 1,260 days equal 3½ years. As half of the perfect number 7, 3½ can indicate incompletion, imperfection, or even evil. Notice the events predicted for this time period: there is trouble (Daniel 12:7), the holy city is trampled (Revelation 11:2), the woman takes refuge in the wilderness (Revelation 12:6), and the Devil-inspired beast exercises his authority (Revelation 13:5). Some commentators link the 3½ years with the period of famine in the days of Elijah (Luke 4:25, James 5:17). Since Malachi predicted the return of Elijah before the Last judgment (Malachi 4:5), and since the events in

Daniel and Revelation pave the way for the second coming, perhaps John was making this connection. It is possible, of course, that the 3½ years are literal. If so, we will clearly recognize when the 3½ years are over! Whether symbolic or literal, however, they indicate that evil's reign will have a definite end.

The beast in Chapter 11:7 could be Satan or an agent of Satan. Jerusalem, once the great city and the capital of Israel is now enemy territory. It is compared with Sodom and with Egypt, both well known for their evil. By the time of John's writing, Jerusalem had been destroyed by the Romans in 70 A.D., nearly a million Jews had been slaughtered, and the Temple treasures had been carried off to Rome.

The whole world rejoices at the deaths of these two witnesses, who have caused trouble by saying what the people did not want to hear—words about their sin, their need for repentance, and the coming punishment. Sinful people hate those who call attention to their sin and who urge them to repent. They hated Christ and they hate his followers, (1 John 3:13). When you obey Christ and take a stand against sin, be prepared to experience the world's hatred. But remember that the great reward awaiting you in heaven far outweighs any suffering you face now.

The seventh trumpet is sounded announcing the arrival of the King. There is now no turning back. The coming judgments are no longer partial but complete in their destruction. God is in control, and He unleashes His full wrath on the evil world that refuses to turn to Him (Chapter 9:20-21). When His wrath begins, there will be no escape.

Who are the 24 elders? Go back to Revelation, Chapter 4:4. In the Bible, God gives rewards to His people according to what they deserve. Throughout the Old Testament, obedience often brought reward in this life (Deuteronomy 28), but obedience and immediate reward are not always linked. If they were, good people would always be rich, and suffering would always be a sign of sin. If we were quickly rewarded for every faithful deed, we would soon think we were rather good. Before long, we would be doing many good deeds for purely selfish reasons. While it is true that God will reward us for our Earthly deeds (Chapter 20:12), our greatest reward will be eternal life in His presence.

In Old Testament days, the Ark of the Covenant was the most sacred treasure of the Israelite nation. Exodus 37:1 explains about the Ark of the Covenant.

NOTES

CHAPTER 12
Observing the Great Conflict

The Woman and the Dragon

The seventh trumpet ushers in the bowl judgments (Chapters 15:1 - 16-21), but in the intervening chapters (12-14), John sees the conflict between God and Satan. He sees the source of all sin, evil, persecution, and suffering on the Earth, and he understands why the great battle between the forces of God and Satan must soon take place. In these chapters the nature of all evil is exposed, and Satan is seen in all his wickedness.

The woman represents God's faithful people who have been waiting for the Messiah; the crown of 12 stars represents the 12 tribes of Israel. God set apart the Jews for Himself (Romans 9:4-5), and that nation gave birth to the Messiah. The boy (Revelation 12:5) is Jesus, born to a devout Jewish girl named Mary (Luke 1:26-33). Evil King Herod immediately tried to destroy the infant Jesus (Matthew 2:13-20). Herod's desire to kill this newborn king, whom he saw as a threat to his throne, was motivated by Satan (the red dragon), who wanted to kill the world's Savior. The heavenly pageant of Revelation 12 shows that Christ's lowly birth in the town of Bethlehem had cosmic significance.

The large red dragon, Satan, has seven heads, ten horns and seven crowns, representing his power and the kingdoms of the world over which he rules. The stars that plunged to Earth with him are usually considered to be the angels who fell with Satan and became his demons. According to Hebrew tradition, one-third of all the angels in heaven fell with Satan.

The wilderness represents a place of spiritual refuge and protection from Satan. Because God aided the woman's escape into the wilderness, we can be sure that He offers security to all true believers. Satan always attacks God's people, but God keeps them spiritually secure. Some will experience physical harm, but all will be protected from spiritual harm. God will not let Satan take the souls of God's true followers. The 1,260 days (3½ years), is the same length of time that the dragon can exercise his authority (Chapter 13:5) and that the holy city is trampled.

The event in verse 7 fulfills Daniel 12:1, Michael is a high-ranking angel. One of his responsibilities is to guard God's community of believers. Much more happened at Christ's birth, death, and resurrection than most people realize.

A war between the forces of good and evil was under way. With Christ's resurrection, Satan's ultimate defeat was assured. Some believe that Satan's fall to Earth took place at Jesus' resurrection or ascension and that the 1,260 days (3½ years) is a symbolic way of referring to the time between Christ's first and second comings. Others say that Satan's defeat will occur in the middle of a literal seven-year tribulation period, following the rapture of the church and preceding the second coming of Christ and the beginning of Christ's 1,000-year reign. Whatever the case, we must remember that Christ is victorious—Satan has already been defeated because of Christ's death on the cross (Chapter 12:10-12).

The Devil is not a symbol or legend, he is very real. Originally Satan was an angel of God, but through his own pride, he became corrupt. Satan is God's enemy and he constantly tried to hinder God's work, but he is limited by God's power and can do only what he is permitted to do (Job 1:6-2:8). The name Satan means "Accuser" (Chapter 12:10). He actively looks for people to attack (1 Peter 5:8-9). Satan likes to pursue believers who are vulnerable in their faith, who are spiritually weak, or who are isolated from other believers.

Even though God permits Satan to do his work in this world, God is still in control. And Jesus has complete control over Satan—He defeated Satan when He died and rose again for the sins of everyone. One day Satan will be bound forever never again to do his evil work (Chapter 20:10). Many believe that until this time, Satan still had access to God. But here his access is forever barred. He can no longer accuse people before God like he did in Job 1:6.

The critical blow to Satan came when the Lamb, Jesus Christ, shed His blood for our sins. The victory is won by sacrifice—Christ's death in our place to pay the penalty for our sin and the sacrifices we make because of our faith in Him. As we face the battle with Satan, we should not fear it or try to escape from it, but we should loyally serve Christ, who alone brings victory (Romans 8:34-39)

Satan begins to step up his persecution because he knows that "he has little time." We are living in the last days and Satan's work has become more intense. Even though Satan is immensely powerful, as we can see by the condition of our world, he is always under God's control. One of the reasons God allows Satan to work evil and bring temptation is so that those who pretend to be Christ's followers will be weeded out from Christ's true believers. Knowing that the last great confrontation with Jesus is near, Satan is desperately trying to recruit as great an enemy force as possible for this final battle.

While the woman (12:1) represents faithful Jews and the child (12:5) represents Christ, the rest of her children could be either Jewish believers or, most likely all believers.

The apostle Paul tells us that we are in a spiritual battle (Ephesians 6:19-12). John says that the war is still being waged, but the outcome has already been determined. Satan and his followers have been defeated and will be destroyed. Nevertheless, Satan is battling daily to bring more into his ranks and to keep his own from defecting to God's side. Those who belong to Christ have gone into battle on God's side, and He has guaranteed them victory. God will not lose the war, but we must make certain not to lose the battle for our own souls. Do not waiver in your commitment to Christ. A great spiritual battle is being fought, and there is no time for indecision.

NOTES

CHAPTER 13
The Beast Out of the Sea

"Then he [the Dragon] stood waiting on the shore of the sea."

This beast was initially identified with Rome because the Roman Empire, in its early days, encouraged an evil lifestyle, persecuted believers, and opposed God and His followers. But the beast also symbolizes the Antichrist, not Satan, but someone under Satan's power and control. This Antichrist looks like a combination of the four beasts that Daniel saw centuries earlier in a vision (Daniel 7). As the dragon (12:17) is in opposition to God, so the beast from the sea is against Christ and may be seen as Satan's false messiah. The early Roman Empire was strong and anti-Christ (or against Christ's standards), many other individual powers throughout history have been anti-Christ. Many Christians believe that Satan's evil will culminate in a final Antichrist; one who will focus all the powers of evil against Jesus Christ and His followers.

This chapter introduces Satan's (the dragon's) two evil accomplices: 1) The beast out of the sea (13:1) and 2) the beast out of the Earth (13:1). Together, the three evil beings form an unholy trinity in direct opposition to the Holy Trinity of God the Father, God the Son, and God the Holy Spirit.

When Satan tempted Jesus in the wilderness, he wanted Jesus to show His power by turning stones into bread, to do miracles by jumping from a high place, and to gain political power by worshipping him (Matthew 4:1-11). Satan's plan was to rule the world through Jesus, but Jesus refused to do Satan's bidding. Thus, Satan turns to the fearsome beasts described in Revelation.

To the beast out of the sea, he gives political power. To the beast out of the Earth, he gives power to do miracles. Both beasts work together to capture the control of the whole world. This unholy trinity—the dragon, the beast out of the sea, and the false prophet (the beast out of the Earth) (Chapter 16:13)—unite in a desperate attempt to overthrow God, but their efforts are doomed to failure. Chapters 19:19-21 and 20:10 tell what becomes of them.

Because the beast, the Antichrist is a false messiah, he will be a counterfeit of Christ and will even stage a false resurrection (13:14). People will follow and worship him because they will be awed by his power and miracles (13:3-4). He will unite the world under his leadership (13:7-8), and he will control the world economy (13:16-17). People are impressed by power and will follow those who display it forcefully or offer it to their followers. But those who follow the beast will only be fooling themselves. He will use his power to manipulate others, to point to himself, and to promote evil plans. God by contrast, uses His infinitely greater power to love and to build up. Do not be misled by claims of great miracles or reports about a resurrection or reincarnation of someone claiming to be Christ. When Jesus returns, He will reveal Himself to everyone (Matthew 24:23-28).

The power given to the beast will be limited by God. He will allow the beast to exercise authority only for a short time. Even while the beast is in power, God will still be in control (Chapters 11:5; and 12:10-12).

The beast will conquer God's people and rule over them, but he will not be able to harm them spiritually. He will establish worldwide dominance and demand that everyone worship him. And many will worship him—everyone except true believers. Refusal to worship the beast will result in temporary suffering for God's people, but they will be rewarded with eternal life in the end.

In this time of persecution, being faithful to Christ could bring imprisonment and even execution. Some believers will be hurt or killed. But all that the beast and his followers will be able to do to believers is harm them physically; no spiritual harm will come to those whose faith in God is sincere. All believers will enter God's presence perfected and purified by the blood of the Lamb (Chapter 7:9-17).

The times of great persecution that John saw will provide an opportunity for believers to exercise patient endurance and faithfulness. The tough times we face right now are also opportunities for spiritual growth. Do not fall into Satan's trap and turn away from God when hard times come. Instead, use those tough times as opportunities for growth.

The first beast came out of the sea, but the second beast comes out of the Earth. Later identified as the false prophet (Chapters 16:13; and 19:20), he is a counterfeit of the Holy Spirit. He seems to do good, but the purpose of his miracles is to deceive.

Throughout the Bible, we see miracles performed as proof of God's power, love, and authority. But here we see counterfeit miracles performed to deceive. This is a reminder of Pharaoh's magicians, who duplicated Moses' signs in Egypt. True signs and miracles point us to Jesus Christ, but miracles alone can be deceptive. That is why we must ask with respect to each miracle we see: Is this consistent with what God says in the Bible? The second beast here gains influence through the signs and wonders that he can perform on behalf of the first beast. The second beast orders the people to worship a statue in honor of the first beast—a direct flouting of the second commandment (Exodus 20:4-6). Allowing the Bible to guide our faith and practice will keep us from being deceived by false signs, however convincing they appear to be. Any teaching that contradicts God's Word is false.

In every generation, Christians need to maintain a healthy skepticism about society's pleasures and rewards. In our educational, economic, and civic structures, there are incentives and rewards. Cooperating Christians must always support what is good and healthy about our society, but we must stand against sin. In some cases, such as Satan's system described here, the system or structure becomes so evil that there is no way to cooperate with it.

This mark of the beast is designed to mock the seal that God places on His followers (Chapter 7:2-3). Just as God marks His people to save them, so Satan's beast marks his people to save them from the persecution that Satan will inflict on God's followers. Identifying this mark is not as important as identifying the purpose of the mark. Those who accept it show their allegiance to Satan, their willingness to operate within the economic system he promotes, and their rebellion against God. To refuse the mark means to commit oneself entirely to God, preferring death to compromising one's faith in Christ.

The meaning of this number has been discussed more than that of any other part of the book of Revelation. The three sixes have been said to represent many things, including the number of a man or the unholy trinity of Satan, the first beast, and the false prophet (Chapter 16:13). If the number seven is considered to be the perfect number in the Bible, and if three sevens represent complete perfection, then the number 666 falls completely short of perfection. The first readers of this book probably applied the number to the emperor Nero, who symbolized all the evils of the Roman Empire. (The Greek letters of Nero's name represent numbers that total 666.) Whatever specific application the number is given, the number symbolizes the worldwide dominion and complete evil of this unholy trinity designed to undo Christ's work and overthrow him.

NOTES

CHAPTER 14
The Lamb and the 144,000

Chapter 13 described the onslaught of evil that will occur when Satan and his helpers control the world. Chapter 14 gives a glimpse into eternity to show believers what awaits them if they endure. The Lamb is the Messiah. Mount Zion, often another name for Jerusalem, the capital of Israel, is contrasted with the worldly empire. The 144,000 represent believers who have endured persecution on Earth and now are ready to enjoy the eternal benefits and blessings of life with God forever. The three angels contrast the destiny of believers with the unbelievers.

These people are true believers whose robes have been washed and made white in Christ's blood (7:14) through His death ("purchased from among the people on the Earth"). In the Old Testament, idolatry was often portrayed as spiritual adultery as described in the book of Hosea. Their purity is best understood symbolically, meaning that they are free from involvement with the pagan world system. These believers are spiritually pure. They have remained faithful to Christ; they have followed Him exclusively and they have received God's reward for staying committed to Him. The "special offering" refers to the act of dedicating the first part (First fruits) of the harvest as holy to God.

Some believe that this is a final, worldwide appeal to all people to recognize the one true God. No one will have the excuse of never hearing God's truth. Others, however, see this as an announcement of judgment rather than as an appeal. The people of the world have had their chance to proclaim their allegiance to God, and now God's great judgment is about to begin. If you are reading this, you have already heard God's truth. You know that God's final judgment will not be put off forever. Have you joyfully received the everlasting Good News? If so, you have nothing to fear from God's judgment. The Judge of all the Earth is your Savior.

Babylon was the name of both an evil city and an immortal empire. A world center for idol worship. Babylon ransacked Jerusalem and carried the people of Judah into captivity (2 Kings 25 and 2 Chronicles 36). Just as Babylon was the Jews' worst enemy, the Roman Empire was the worst enemy of the early Christians. John, who probably did not dare speak against Rome openly, applied the name Babylon to this enemy of God's people (Rome)—and, by extension, to all God's enemies of all times.

Those who worship the beast, accept his mark on their foreheads, and operate according to his world economic system will ultimately face God's judgment. Our world values money, power, and pleasure over God's leadership. To get what the world values, many people deny God and violate Christian principles. Thus, they must drink of the wine of God's wrath (Psalm 75; Isaiah 51:17).

The ultimate result of sin is unending separation from God. Because human beings are created in God's image with an inborn thirst for fellowship with Him, separation from God will be the ultimate torment and misery. Sin always brings misery, but in this life, we can choose to repent and restore our relationship with God. In eternity there will no longer be opportunity for repentance. If in this life we choose to be independent of God, in the next life we will be separated from Him forever. Nobody is forced to choose eternal separation from God, and nobody suffers this fate by accident. Jesus invites all of us to open the door of our heart to Him. If we do this, we will enjoy everlasting fellowship with Him.

The news about God's ultimate triumph should encourage God's people to remain faithful through every trial and persecution. They can do this, God promises, by trusting in Jesus and obeying the commands found in His Word. The secret to enduring therefore, is trust and obedience. Trust God to give you patience to endure even the small trials you face daily, obey Him even when obedience is unattractive or dangerous.

While it is true that money, fame, and belongings cannot be taken with us from this life, God's people can provide fruit that survives even death. God will remember our love, kindness, and faithfulness, and those who accept Christ through our witness will join us in the new Earth. Be sure that your values are in line with God's values and decide today to produce fruit that lasts forever.

This is an image of judgment: Christ is separating the fruitful from the unfaithful like a farmer harvesting his crops. This is a time of joy for the Christians who have been persecuted and martyred—they will receive their long-awaited reward. Christians should not fear the Last Judgment. Jesus said, "I assure you, those who listen to my message and believe in God who sent me have eternal life. They will never be condemned for their sins, but they have already passed from death into life" (John 5:24).

A winepress was a large vat or trough where grapes were collected and then crushed. The juice flowed out of a duct that led into a large holding vat. The winepress is often used in the Bible as a symbol of God's wrath and judgment against sin (Isaiah 63:3-6; Lamentations 1:15; Joel 3:12-13).

The distance of 180 miles is approximately the north-south length of Palestine.

NOTES

CHAPTER 15
Pouring Out the Seven Plagues

The Song of Moses and of the Lamb

The seven last plagues are also called the seven bowl judgments. They begin in Chapter 16. Unlike the previous plagues, these are universal, and they will culminate in the abolition of all evil and the end of the world.

This is similar to the "sea of glass" described in 4:6, located before the throne of God. Here it is mixed with fire to represent wrath and judgment. Those who stand beside it are victorious over Satan and his evil beast.

The song of Moses celebrated Israel's deliverance from Egypt (Exodus 15). The song of the Lamb celebrates the ultimate deliverance of God's people from the power of Satan.

This imagery brings us back to the time of the Exodus in the wilderness when the Ark of the Covenant (the symbol of God's presence among His people) resided in the Tabernacle. The angels coming out of the Temple are clothed in spotless white linen with gold belts across their chests. Their garments reminiscent of the high priest's clothing, show that they are free from corruption, immorality, and injustice. The smoke that fills the Temple is the manifestation of God's glory and power. There is no escape from this judgment. Our eternal reign with Christ will not begin until all evil is destroyed by His judgment. The fruitful must wait for His timetable to be revealed.

NOTES

CHAPTER 16
The Seven Bowls of the Seven Plagues

The bowl judgments are God's final and complete judgments on the Earth. The end has come. There are many similarities between the bowl judgments and the trumpet judgments (8:6-11:19), but there are three main differences: 1) These judgments are complete whereas the trumpet judgments are partial; 2) the trumpet judgments still give unbelievers the opportunity to repent, but the bowl judgments do not; and 3) people are indirectly affected by several of the trumpet judgments but directly attacked by all the bowl judgments.

The significance of the altar itself responding is that everyone and everything will be praising God, acknowledging His righteousness and perfect justice.

We know that the people realize that these judgments come from God because they curse Him for sending them. But they still refuse to recognize God's authority and repent of their sins. Christians should not be surprised at the hostility and hardness of heart of unbelievers. Even when the power of God is fully and completely revealed, many will still refuse to repent. If you find yourself ignoring God more and more, turn back to Him now before your heart becomes too hard to repent.

The Euphrates River was a natural protective boundary against the empires to the east (Babylon, Assyria, Persia). If it dried up, nothing could hold back invading armies. The armies to the east symbolize unhindered judgment.

These evil spirits performing miraculous signs, who come out of the mouths of the unholy trinity, unite the rulers of the world for battle against God. The imagery of the demons coming out of the mouths of the three evil rulers signifies the verbal enticements and propaganda that will draw many people to their evil cause.

Christ will return unexpectedly (1 Thessalonians 5:1-6), so we must be ready when He returns. We can prepare ourselves by standing firm in temptation and by being committed to God's moral standards. In what ways does your life show either your readiness or your lack of preparation for Christ's return?

This battlefield called Armageddon is near the city of Megiddo (southeast of the modern port of Haifa), which guarded a large plain in northern Israel. It is a strategic location near a prominent international highway leading north from Egypt through Israel, along the coast, and on to Babylon. Megiddo overlooked the entire plain southward toward Galilee and westward to the mountains of Gilboa.

Sinful people will unite to fight against God in a final display of rebellion. Many are already united against Christ and His people—those who stand for truth, peace, justice, and morality. Your personal battle with evil foreshadows the great battle pictured here, where God will meet evil and destroy it once and for all. Be strong and courageous as you battle against sin and evil: You are fighting on the winning side.

Babylon's division into three sections is a symbol of its complete destruction.

NOTES

CHAPTER 17
Seizing the Final Victory
The Great Prostitute

The destruction of Babylon mentioned in 16:17-21 is now described in greater detail. The "great prostitute," called Babylon, represents the early Roman Empire with its many gods, and the blood of Christian martyrs on its hands. The water stands for either sea commerce or a well-watered (well-provisioned) city. The great prostitute represents the seductiveness of the governmental system that uses immoral means to gain its own pleasure, prosperity, and advantage. In contrast to the prostitute, Christ's bride, the church, is pure and obedient (19:6-9). The wicked city of Babylon contrasts with the heavenly city of Jerusalem (21:10-22:5). The original readers probably rather quickly identified Babylon with Rome. But Babylon also symbolizes any system that is hostile to God.

The scarlet beast is either the dragon of 12:3 or the beast out of the sea described in 13:1.

Throughout history, people have been killed for their faith. Over the last century, millions have been killed by oppressive governments, and many of those victims were believers. The woman's drunkenness shows her pleasure in her evil accomplishments and her false feeling of triumph over the church. But every martyr who has fallen before her sword has only served to strengthen the faith of the church.

In chapter 12, we met the dragon (Satan). In chapter 13 we saw the beast from the sea and the power he received from Satan. In chapters 14-16 we see God's great judgments. In this chapter, a scarlet beast like the beast and the dragon appears as an ally of the great prostitute. The beast was alive, died, and then came back to life. The beast's resurrection symbolizes the persistence of evil. This resurgence of evil power will convince many to join forces with the beast, but those who choose the side of evil condemn themselves to the Devil's fate—eternal torment.

In verses 9-11, John is referring to Rome, the city famous for its seven hills. Many say that this city also symbolized all evil in the world—any person, religion, group, government, or structure that opposed Christ. Whatever view is taken of the seven hills and seven kings, this section indicates the climax of Satan's struggle against God. Evil's power is limited, and its destruction is on the horizon.

The 10 horns represent kings of nations yet to arise. Rome will be followed by other powers. Rome is a good example of how the Antichrist's system will work, demanding complete allegiance and ruling by raw power, oppression, and slavery. Whoever the 10 kings are, they will give their power to the Antichrist and make war against the Lamb.

In a dramatic turn of events, the prostitute's allies turn on her and destroy her. This is how evil operates. Destructive by its very nature, it discards its own adherents when they cease to serve its purposes. An unholy alliance is an uneasy alliance because each partner puts its own interests first.

No matter what happens, we must trust that God is still in charge, that God overrules all the plans and intrigues of the evil one, and that God's plans will happen just as he says. God even uses people opposed to him as tools to execute His will. Although He allows evil to permeate this present world, the new Earth will never know sin.

NOTES

CHAPTER 18
The Fall of Babylon

This chapter shows the complete destruction of Babylon, John's metaphorical name for the evil world power and all it represents. Everything that tries to block God's purposes will come to a violent end.

Merchants in the Roman Empire grew rich by exploiting the sinful pleasures of their society. Many businesspeople today do the same thing. Businesses and governments are often based on greed, money, and power. Many bright individuals are tempted to take advantage of an evil system to enrich themselves. Christians are warned to stay free from the lure of money, status, and the good life. We are to live according to the values Christ exemplified: service, giving, self-sacrifice, obedience, and truth.

The people of Babylon had lived in luxury and pleasure. The city boasted, "I am queen on my throne. . .. I will not experience sorrow." The powerful, wealthy people of this world are susceptible to this same attitude. A person who is financially comfortable often feels invulnerable, secure, and in control, feeling no need for God or anyone else. This kind of attitude defies God, and His judgment against it is harsh. We are told to avoid Babylon's sins. If you are financially secure, do not become complacent and deluded by the myth of self-sufficiency. Use your resources to help others and advance God's Kingdom.

Those who are tied to the world's system will lose everything when it collapses. What they have worked for a lifetime to build up will be destroyed in one hour. Those who work only for material rewards will have nothing when they die or when their possessions are destroyed. What can we take with us to the new Earth? Our faith, our Christian character, and our relationships with other believers. These are more important than any amount of money, power, or pleasure.

Those who are in control of various parts of the economic system will mourn at Babylon's fall. The political leaders will mourn because they were the overseers of Babylon's wealth and were able to enrich themselves greatly. The merchants will mourn because Babylon, the greatest customer for their goods, will be gone. The sea captains will no longer have anywhere to bring their goods because the merchants will have nowhere to sell them. The fall of the evil world system affects all who enjoyed and depended on it. No one will remain unaffected by Babylon's fall.

This list of various merchandise illustrates the extreme materialism of this society. Few of these goods are necessities—most are luxuries. The society had become so self-indulgent that people were willing to use evil means to gratify their desires. Even people had become commodities—people were sold as slaves to Babylon.

God's people should not live for money, because money will be worthless in eternity. And they should keep on guard constantly against greed, a sin that is always ready to take over their lives.

NOTES

CHAPTER 19
Songs of Victory in Heaven

Praise is the heartfelt response to God by those who love Him. The more you get to know God and realize what He has done, the more you will respond with praise. Praise is at the heart of true worship. Let your praise of God flow out of your realization of who He is and how much He loves you.

A vast crown in heaven initiates the chorus of praise to God for His victory (19:1-3). Then the 24 elders join the chorus. Finally, the great choir of heaven once again praises God—the wedding of the Lamb has come (19:6-8).

This is the culmination of human history—the judgment of the wicked and the wedding of the Lamb and His bride, the church. The church consists of all faithful believers from all time. The bride's clothing stands in sharp contrast to the gaudy clothing of the great prostitute of 17:4 and 18:16. The bride's clothing represents the good deeds of the believers. These good deeds are not done by believers to their merit, but they reflect the work of Christ to save us (7:9,14).

The angel did not accept John's homage and worship because only God is worthy of worship. Like John, it would be easy for us to become overwhelmed by this prophetic pageant. But Jesus is the central focus of God's revelation and His redemptive plan. As you read the book of Revelation, do not get bogged down in all the details of the awesome visions; remember that the overarching theme in all the visions is the ultimate victory of Jesus Christ over evil.

The Rider on the White Horse

The name "Faithful and True" contrasts with the faithless and deceitful Babylon described in chapter 18.

John's vision shifts again. Heaven opens, and Jesus appears—this time not as a Lamb but as a warrior on a white horse (symbolizing victory). Jesus came first as a Lamb to be a sacrifice for sin, but He will return as a conqueror and king to execute judgment (2 Thessalonians 1:7-10). Jesus' first coming brought forgiveness; His second will bring judgment. The battle lines have been drawn between God and evil, and the world is waiting for the King to ride onto the field.

Although Jesus is called "Faithful and True" (19:11), "Word of God" (19:13), and "King of Kings and Lord of Lords: (19:16), this verse implies that no name can do Him justice. He is greater than any description or expression the human mind can devise.

In verse 16, this title indicates our God's sovereignty. Most of the world is worshiping the beast, the antichrist, whom they believe has all power and authority. Then suddenly out of heaven ride Christ and His army of angels—the "King of Kings and Lord of Lords." His entrance signals the end of the false powers.

The battle lines have been drawn, and the greatest confrontation in the history of the world is about to begin. The beast (the Antichrist) and the false prophet have gathered the governments and armies of the Earth under the Antichrist's rule. The enemy armies believe they have come of their own volition; in reality, God has summoned them to battle to defeat them. That they would even presume to fight against God shows how their pride and rebellion have distorted their thinking. There really is no fight, however, because the victory was won when Jesus died on the cross for sin and rose from the dead. Thus, the evil leaders are immediately captured and sent to their punishment, and the forces of evil are annihilated.

The lake of fire that burns with sulfur is the final destination of the wicked. This lake is different from the bottomless pit referred to in Chapter 9:1. The Antichrist and the false prophet are thrown into the lake of fire. Then their leader, Satan himself, will be thrown into that lake (20:10), and finally death and the grave (20:14). Afterward, everyone whose name is not recorded in the Book of Life will be thrown into the lake of fire (20:15).

NOTES

CHAPTER 20
The Thousand Years

The angel and the bottomless pit are explained in Chapters 9:1 and 19:20.

The dragon, Satan, is discussed in more detail in Chapters 12:3-4 and 12:9. The dragon is not bound as punishment—but so that he cannot deceive the nations.

The 1,000 years are often referred to as the Millennium (Latin for 1,000). Just how and when this 1,000-year period takes place is understood differently among Christian scholars. The three major positions on this issue are postmillennialism, premillennialism, Amillennialism.

1) Postmillennialism looks for a literal 1,000-year period of peace on Earth ushered in by the church. At the end of the 1,000 years, Satan will be unleashed once more, but then Christ will return to defeat him and reign forever. Christ's second coming will not occur until after the 1,000-year period.
2) Premillennialism also views the 1,000 years as a literal time period but holds that Christ's second coming initiates His 1,000-year reign and that this reign occurs before the final removal of Satan.
3) Amillennialism understands the 1,000-year period to be symbolic of the time between Christ's ascension and His return. This Millennium is the reign of Christ in the hearts of believers and in His church, thus, it is another way of

referring to the 'church age'. This period will end with the second coming of Christ.

These different views about the Millennium need not cause division and controversy in the church because each view acknowledges what is most crucial to Christianity: Christ will return, defeat Satan, and reign forever! Whatever and whenever the Millennium is, Jesus Christ will unite all believers; therefore, we should not let this issue divide us.

John does not say why God once again sets Satan free, but it is part of God's plan for judging the world. Perhaps it is to expose those who rebel against God in their hearts and confirm those who are truly faithful to God. Whatever the reason, Satan's release results in the final destruction of all evil.

Christians hold two basic views concerning this first resurrection:
1) Some believe that the first resurrection is spiritual (in our heart at salvation) and that the Millennium is our spiritual reign with Christ between His first and second comings. During this time, we are priests of God because Christ reigns in our hearts. In this view, the second resurrection is the bodily resurrection of all people for judgment.
2) Others believe that the first resurrection occurs after Satan has been set aside. It is a physical resurrection of believers, who then reign with Christ on the Earth for a literal 1,000 years. The second resurrection occurs at the end of this Millennium to judge unbelievers who have died.

The second death is spiritual death—everlasting separation from God (Chapter 21:8).

The Defeat of Satan

Gog and Magog symbolize all the forces of evil that band together to battle God. Noah's son Japheth had a son named Magog (Genesis 10:2). Ezekiel presents Gog as a leader of forces against Israel (Ezekiel 38-39).

This is not a typical battle where the outcome is in doubt during the heat of the conflict. Here there is no contest. Two mighty forces of evil—those of the beast (19:19) and of Satan (20:8)—unite to do battle against God. The Bible uses just two verses to describe each battle: The evil beast and his forces are captured and thrown into the lake of fire (19:20-21), and fire from heaven devours Satan and his attacking armies (20:9-10). For God, it is as easy as that. There will be no doubt, no worry, no second thoughts for believers about whether they have chosen the right side. If you are with God, you will experience this tremendous victory with Christ.

The Final Judgment

Satan's power is not eternal—he will meet his doom. He began his evil work in people at the beginning (Genesis 3:1-6) and continues it today, but he will be destroyed when he is thrown into the lake of fire. The Devil will be released from the bottomless pit ("his prison," 20:7), but he will never be released from the lake of fire. He will never be a threat to anyone again

At the judgment, the books are opened. They represent God's judgment, and in them are recorded the deeds of everyone, good or evil. We are not saved by deeds, but deeds are clear evidence of a person's actual relationship with God. The Book of Life contains the names of those who have put their trust in Christ to save them.

Death and the grave are thrown into the lake of fire. God's judgment is finished. The lake of fire is the ultimate destination of everything wicked—Satan, the beast, the false prophet, the demons, death, the grave, and all those whose names are not recorded in the Book of Life because they did not place their faith in Jesus Christ. John's vision does not permit any gray areas in God's judgment. If by faith we have not identified with Christ, confessing Him as Lord, there will be no hope, no second chance, no other appeal.

NOTES

CHAPTER 21
Making All Things New

The New Jerusalem

The Earth as we know it will not last forever, but after God's great judgment, He will create a new Earth (Romans 8:18-21; 2 Peter 3:7-13). God had also promised Isaiah that He would create a new and eternal Earth (Isaiah 65:17 and 66:22). The sea in John's time was viewed as dangerous and changeable. It was also the source of the beast (13:1). We do not know how the new Earth will look or where it will be, but God and His followers—those whose names are written in the Book of Life—will be united to live there forever. Will you be there?

The new Jerusalem is where God lives among His people. Instead of our going up to meet Him, He comes down to be with us, just as God became man in Jesus Christ and lived among us (John 1:14). Wherever God reigns, there is peace, security, and love.

Have you ever wondered what eternity will be like? The "Holy City, the New Jerusalem" is described as the place where God will "remove all. . .sorrows." Forevermore, there will be no death, sorrow, crying, or pain. What a wonderful truth! No matter what you are going through, it is not the last word—God has written the final chapter, and it is about true fulfillment and eternal joy for those who love Him. We do not know as much as we would like, but it is enough to know that eternity with God will be more wonderful than we could ever imagine.

God is the Creator. The Bible begins with the majestic story of His creation of the Universe, and it concludes with His creation of a new heaven and a new Earth. This is a tremendous hope and encouragement for the believer. When we are with God, with our sins forgiven and our future secure, we will be like Christ. We will be made perfect like Him.

Just as God finished the work of creation (Genesis 2:1-3) and Jesus finished the work of redemption (John 19:30), so the Trinity will finish the entire plan of salvation by inviting the redeemed into a new creation.

The "cowards" are not those who are fainthearted in their faith or who sometimes doubt or question but those who turn back from following God. They are not brave enough to stand up for Christ; they are not humble enough to accept His authority over their lives. They are put in the same list as the unbelieving, the corrupt, the murderers, the immoral, the idolaters, the liars, and those practicing magic arts.

People who are victorious "endure to the end" (Mark 13:13). They will receive the blessings that God promised:
    1) eating from the tree of Life (Revelation 2:7)
    2) escaping from the lake of fire (the "second death", Revelation 2:11)
    3) receiving a special name (Revelation 2:17)
    4) having authority over the nations (Revelation 2:26
    5) being included in the Book of Life (Revelation 3:5)
    6) being a pillar in God's spiritual temple (Revelation 3:12)
    7) sitting with Christ on His throne (Revelation 3:21)

Those who can endure the testing of evil and remain faithful will be rewarded by God.

The second death is a spiritual death, meaning either eternal torment or destruction. In either case, it is permanent separation from God.

The rest of the chapter is a stunning description of the new City of God. The vision is symbolic and shows us that our new home with God will defy description. We will not be disappointed in it in any way.

The new Jerusalem is a picture of God's future home for His people. The 12 tribes of Israel (21:12) probably represent all the faithful in the Old Testament; the 12 apostles (21:14) represent the church. Thus, both believing Gentiles and Jews who have been faithful to God will live together in the new Earth.

The City's measurements are symbolic of a place that will hold all God's people. These measurements are all multiples of 12, the number for God's people. There were 12 tribes in Israel, and 12 apostles who started the church. The walls are 144 (12 x 12) cubits (200 feet) thick; there are 12 layers in the walls, and 12 gates in the city; and the height, length, and breadth, are all the same, 12,000 stadia (1400 miles). The new Jerusalem is a perfect cube, the same shape as the Most Holy Place in the Temple (1Kings 6:20). These measurements illustrate that this new home will be perfect for us.

The picture of walls made of jewels reveals that the new Jerusalem will be a place of purity and durability—it will last forever.

The Temple, the center of God's presence among his people was the primary place of worship. No temple is needed in the new city, however, because God's presence will be everywhere. He will be worshiped throughout the city, and nothing will hinder us from being with Him.

Not everyone will be allowed into the new Jerusalem, but "only those whose names are written in the Lamb's Book of Life." Do not think that you will get in because of your background, personality, or good behavior. Eternal life is available to you only because of what Jesus, the Lamb, has done. Trust Him today to secure your citizenship in His new creation.

NOTES

CHAPTER 22

The water of life is a symbol of eternal life. Jesus used the same image with the Samaritan woman (John 4:7-14). It pictures the fullness of life with God and the eternal blessings that come when we believe in Him and allow Him to satisfy our spiritual thirst (22:17).

The tree of life is like the tree of life in the Garden of Eden (Genesis 2:9). After Adam and Eve sinned, they were forbidden to eat from the tree of life because they could not have eternal life if they were under sin's control. But because of the forgiveness of sin through the blood of Jesus, there will be no evil or sin in this city. We will be able to eat freely from the tree of life when sin's control over us is destroyed and our eternity with God is secure.

Why would the nations need to be healed if all evil is gone? John is quoting from Ezekiel 47:12, where water flowing from the Temple produces trees with healing leaves. He is not implying that there will be illness in the new Earth; he is emphasizing that the water of life produces health and strength wherever it goes.

"No longer will anything be cursed" means that nothing accursed will be in God's presence. This fulfills Zechariah's prophecy (Zechariah 14:11).

Hearing or reading an eyewitness account is the next best thing to seeing the event yourself. John witnessed the events reported in Revelation and wrote them down so we could see and believe as he did. If you have read this far, you have seen. Have you also believed?

Jesus is Coming

The first of the Ten Commandments is "Do not worship any other gods besides me" (Exodus 20:3). Jesus said that the greatest command of Moses' law was "You must love the Lord your God with all your heart, all your soul, and all your mind" (Matthew 22:37). Here, at the end of the Bible, this truth is reiterated. The angel instructs John to "worship God!" God alone is worthy of our worship and adoration. He is above all creation even the angels. Are there people, ideas, goals, or possessions that occupy the central place in your life, crowding God out? Worship only God by allowing nothing to distract you from your devotion to Him.

The angel tells John what to do after his vision is over. Instead of sealing up what he has written, as Daniel was commanded to do, (Daniel 12:4-12), the book is to be left open so that all can read and understand. Daniel's message was sealed because it was not a message for Daniel's time. But the book of Revelation was a message for John's time, and it is relevant today. As Christ's return gets closer, there is a greater polarization between God's followers and Satan's followers. We must read the book of Revelation, hear its message, and be prepared for Christ's imminent return.

Those who wash their robes are those who seek to purify themselves from a sinful way of life. They strive daily to remain faithful and ready for Christ's return.

In Eden, Adam and Eve were barred from any access to the tree of life because of their sin (Genesis 3:22-24). In the new Earth, God's people will eat from the tree of life because their sins have been removed by Christ's death and resurrection. Those who eat from the tree will live forever. If Jesus has forgiven your sins, you will have the right to eat from this tree.

The exact location of these sinners is not known, nor is it relevant. They are outside. They were judged and condemned in 21:8. The emphasis is that nothing evil and no sinner will be in God's presence to corrupt or harm any of the faithful.

Jesus is both David's "source" and "heir." As the Creator of all, Jesus existed long before David. As a human, however, He was one of David's direct descendants (Isaiah 11:1-5; Matthew 1:1-17). As the Messiah, He is the "bright morning star," the light of salvation to all.

Both the Holy Spirit and the bride, the church, extend the invitation to all the world to come to Jesus and experience the joys of salvation in Christ.

When Jesus met the Samaritan woman at the well, He told her of the living water that He could supply (John 4:10-15). This image is used again as Christ invites anyone to come and drink of the water of life. The Good News is unlimited in scope—all people everywhere may come. Salvation cannot be earned, but God gives it freely. We live in a world desperately thirsty for living water, and many are dying of thirst. But it is still not too late. Let us invite everyone to come and drink.

We do not know the day or the hour, but Jesus is coming soon and unexpectedly. This is good news to those who trust Him, but a terrible message for those who have rejected Him and stand under His judgment. Soon means "at any moment," and we must be ready for Him, always prepared for His return. Would Jesus' sudden appearance catch you off guard?

NOTES

CONCLUSION

The warning in chapter 22 verse 18, is given to those who might purposefully distort the message in this book. Moses gave a similar warning in Deuteronomy 4:1-4. We, too, must handle the Bible with care and great respect so that we do not distort its message, even unintentionally. We should be quick to put its principles into practice in our life. No human explanation or interpretation of God's Word should be elevated to the same authority as the text itself.

Revelation is, above all a book of hope. It shows that no matter what happens on Earth, God is in control. It promises that evil will not last forever and it depicts the wonderful reward that is waiting for all those who believe in Jesus Christ as Savior and Lord.

Revelation closes human history as Genesis opened it—in paradise. But there is one distinct difference in Revelation—evil is gone forever. Genesis describes Adam and Eve walking and talking with God; Revelation describes people worshiping God face to face. Genesis describes a garden with an evil serpent; Revelation describes a perfect city with no evil. The Garden of Eden is destroyed by sin; but paradise is re-created in the new Jerusalem.

The book of Revelation ends with an urgent plea: "Come, Lord Jesus!" In a world of problems, persecution, evil and immorality, Christ calls us to endure in our faith. Our efforts to better our world are important, but their results cannot compare with the transformation that Jesus will bring about when He returns. He alone controls human history, forgives sin, and will recreate the Earth and bring lasting peace.

NOTES

Final Blessing

"The grace of the Lord Jesus be with you all.
Amen."
Revelation 22:21

vi

www.ingramcontent.com/pod-product-compliance
Lightning Source LLC
Chambersburg PA
CBHW080405170426
43193CB00016B/2817